Cool Hotels
Cool Prices

teNeues

Imprint

Produced by fusion publishing GmbH, Berlin   www.fusion-publishing.com

Edited by Patricia Massó, fusion publishing
Editorial coordination by Bettina Schlösser, teNeues Verlag, Manuela Roth, fusion publishing; Text by Patricia Massó; Translations by Wohanka & Kollegen; Layout by Manuela Roth; Pre-press & imaging by fusion publishing

Cover photo (location): courtesy of Shanghai Mansion (Shanghai Mansion Bangkok)
Back cover photos from top to bottom (location): courtesy of Shanghai Mansion (Shanghai Mansion Bangkok), Christoph Kraneburg (The Square), Roland Bauer (Hotel misc), Douglas Lyle Thompson and Jon Johnson (ACE Hotel Palm Springs), courtesy of Riad 72 (Riad 72)

Photos (location): Marcus Bachmann (The Hatton), Roland Bauer (Warwick Barsey Hotel, Hotel misc, Hotel La Maison, Hotel Chelsea, Bourg Tibourg), Jeff Caven (Hotel St. Francis p. 32, 34), Kate Russell (Hotel St. Francis p. 33, 35, 36), Richard Cerf RiCe (La Maison Bordeaux), Courtesy of ACE Hotel (ACE Hotel Seattle, p. 5 right), courtesy of Arthotel Blaue Gans (Blaue Gans), courtesy of Bo Bo (Bo Bo), courtesy of Casa della Palma (Casa della Palma), courtesy of dusitD2 chiang mai (dusitD2 chiang mai), courtesy of Firmdale Hotels (Knightsbridge Hotel), courtesy of Goldman 25h, www.designhotels.com (Goldmann 25Hours), courtesy of Grand Daddy (Grand Daddy), courtesy of Hotel Amano (Hotel Amano), courtesy of Media One Hotel (Media One Hotel Dubai), courtesy of Rex Hotel (Rex Hotel), courtesy of Riad 72 (Riad 72, p. 6 right), courtesy of ROOM MATE HOTELS (Room Mate Oscar), courtesy of Shanghai Mansion (Shanghai Mansion, p. 7 left), courtesy of Solar do Castelo (Solar do Castelo), courtesy of South Beach Group (Catalina Hotel & Beach Club), courtesy of The Mosaic Hotel (Mosaic), courtesy of The Standard, Downtown LA (The Standard Downtown LA, p. 8 left), Courtesy of The Standard, New York (The Standard New York), courtesy of Vibe Hotel Sydney (Vibe Hotel Sydney, p. 7 right), Douglas Lyle Thompson and Jon Johnson (ACE Hotel Palm Springs, p. 8 right), Alissa Dragun (Hotel Biba), Michelle Galindo (Hotel Soho Barcelona), Gavin Jackson (Pousada Picinguaba, Main House, Ajia Hotel), Joie de Vivre Hotels (Good Hotel), Christoph Kraneburg (The Square), Pascale Lauber (Jardin D'ébène), Undine Pröhl courtesy of HABITA MTY (Habita Monterrey p. 9 left, 54, 55, 58, 59), Adrien Dirand courtesy of HABITA MTY (Habita Monterrey p. 56-57), Undine Pröhl, courtesy of CONDESAdf (CONDESAdf), Jörg Tietje (Townhouse 12), Timon Wehrli (JIA Shanghai p. 190, 192), Reto Guntli (JIA Shanghai p. 191), Michael Weber (JIA Shanghai p. 194, 195), Timon Wehrli of Red Dog Studio (JIA Hong Kong p. 184, 186-189), Grischa Ruschendorf (JIA Hong Kong p. 185)

Price orientation: $ = < 150 $, $$ = 151 $ − 250 $

Published by teNeues Publishing Group

teNeues Verlag GmbH + Co. KG
Am Selder 37
47906 Kempen, Germany
Tel.: 0049-(0)2152-916-0
Fax: 0049-(0)2152-916-111
E-mail: books@teneues.de

teNeues Publishing Company
16 West 22nd Street
New York, NY 10010, USA
Tel.: 001-212-627-9090
Fax: 001-212-627-9511

teNeues Publishing UK Ltd.
21 Marlowe Court, Lymer Avenue
London, SE19 1LP
Great Britain
Tel.: 0044-208-670-7522
Fax: 0044-208-670-7523

teNeues France S.A.R.L.
39, rue de Billets
18250 Henrichemont
France
Tel.: 0033-2-48269348
Fax: 0033-1-70723482

Press department: arehn@teneues.de
Tel.: 0049-(0)2152-916-202

www.teneues.com

ISBN: 978-3-8327-9398-2

© 2010 teNeues Verlag GmbH + Co. KG, Kempen

Printed in China

Bibliographic information published by Die Deutsche Nationalbibliothek.
Die Deutsche Nationalbibliothek lists this publication in the Deutsche Nationalbibliografie; detailed bibliographic data is available in the Internet at http://dnb.d-nb.de.

Contents   Page

Introduction

There are many affordable hotels. However, anyone who expects more than merely a cheap overnight accommodation for two days and is also looking for something special while travelling, sets their standards not only according to price alone.

Fortunately there are affordable hotels in which you can immerse yourself in a very special atmosphere immediately upon entry and easily acquaint yourself with your surroundings. Often, these are smaller privately run hotels whose owners have personally characterised the style of the accommodations. The *Jardin D'ébène* in Cape Town was discovered by its present-day owner during a holiday trip and the passion for this project is reflected in all its details. The *Chelsea* in Cologne houses original works by contemporary artists, with which the owner is personally connected.

But more often it is the hotel groups which have specialised in the "price-friendly" hotel segment and are lined up to fulfill the new demands of their clientele: the desire for originality and a certain feel-good factor, away from the all-too-cool design and anonymity of more favourably priced chain hotels without any charm. The individual establishments of these new hotel groups such as the *ACE Hotel Palm Springs* and the *Hotel Oscar* of the Spanish Room Mate hotel group have been designed individually to take into account their relationships with their respective environments. The rooms within the individual hotels do not even have the same furnishings.

The concepts underlying these hotels are very different. But they have one thing in common – their respective and distinct characters.

Alex Calderwood, one of the founders and creative minds behind the ACE hotel group based in Seattle, brings his strategy down to an even simpler denominator: "simple, basic, comfortable." However this assertion seems to be understated in view of the services offered. Whoever fears that they will not receive the same service for a downgraded price is mistaken, for free WIFI, room service, small restaurants and hip bars, are not a rarity in these hotels.

"All of life is problem solving": this is an old philosophical realisation. And every solution is an opportunity for improvement.

It seems that there has been a remarkable improvement in the hotel industry. Whoever would like their hotel stay to be an unforgettable experience without having to pay a small fortune, has a good chance of getting what they desire.

Patricia Massó

Einleitung

Bezahlbare Hotels gibt es viele. Wer aber mehr erwartet, als einfach nur eine günstige Übernachtungsmöglichkeit zwischen zwei Terminen und auch auf Reisen stets auf der Suche nach dem Besonderen ist, der setzt seine Maßstäbe nicht nur nach dem Preis.

Zum Glück gibt es sie – bezahlbare Hotels, in denen man bereits beim Eintreten in eine ganz besondere Atmosphäre eintaucht und auf Anhieb mit seinem Wohnsitz auf Zeit Freundschaft schließt. Oft sind es die kleineren, privat geführten Hotels, deren Besitzer den Stil des Hauses persönlich geprägt haben, wie das *Jardin D'ébène* in Kapstadt, das von seinen heutigen Eigentümerinnen während eines Urlaubstrips entdeckt wurde und in dem sich die Passion für dieses Projekt in allen Details widerspiegelt, oder das *Chelsea* in Köln, in dem überall Originalwerke zeitgenössischer Künstler hängen, mit denen der Eigentümer persönlich in Verbindung steht. Mehr und mehr sind es aber auch Hotelgruppen, die sich auf das „preisfreundliche" Hotelsegment spezialisiert haben und angetreten sind, den neuen Ansprüchen ihrer Klientel gerecht zu werden: Dem Wunsch nach Originalität und einem gewissen Wohlfühlfaktor, weg von allzu kühlem Design und der Anonymität günstiger Kettenhotels ohne jeden Charme. Den einzelnen Häusern dieser neuen Hotelgruppen, wie z.B. dem *ACE Hotel Palm Springs* oder dem *Hotel Oscar* der spanischen *Room Mate* Hotelgruppe, sieht man ihre Zusammengehörigkeit nur noch bedingt an, da sie ganz individuell und unter Beachtung des Bezugs zu ihrer jeweiligen Umgebung konzipiert wurden. Nicht einmal die Zimmer eines einzelnen Hotels haben die gleiche Ausstattung. Die diesen Hotels zugrunde liegenden Konzepte sind ganz unterschiedlich. Aber sie haben eines gemeinsam – den jeweils ganz eigenen Charakter. Alex Calderwood, einer der Gründer und Kreativen der in Seattle ansässigen ACE Hotelgruppe, bringt seine Strategie auf einen noch einfacheren Nenner: „Simple, basic, comfortable". Allerdings erscheint diese Aussage in Anbetracht der angebotenen Leistungen untertrieben. Wer befürchtet, zum abgespeckten Preis auch nur einen ebensolchen Service erwarten zu dürfen, irrt. Kostenloses WIFI, Room Service, kleine Restaurants und angesagte Bars sind in diesen Hotels keine Seltenheit.

„Alles Leben ist Problemlösen" – dies ist eine alte philosophische Erkenntnis. Und jede Lösung verheißt eine Verbesserung.

Es scheint, auch in der Hotellerie haben wir eine bemerkenswerte Verbesserung zu verzeichnen. Wer seinen Hotelaufenthalt gerne auch einem unvergesslichen Erlebnis gleichsetzen möchte, ohne dafür ein kleines Vermögen zu bezahlen, hat heutzutage die allerbesten Chancen.

Patricia Massó

Introduction

Il existe beaucoup d'hôtels abordables. Si l'on attend cependant plus qu'une simple solution pour passer la nuit entre deux rendez-vous et si l'on recherche constamment l'exception en voyage, on ne porte ses exigences pas seulement sur le prix. Heureusement, il existe des hôtels abordables, dans lesquels l'on plonge dans une atmosphère toute particulière dès que l'on en franchit le seuil, et où l'on se lie immédiatement d'amitié avec sa résidence temporaire. Il s'agit souvent de petits hôtels particuliers, dont les propriétaires ont marqué personnellement le style de la maison, tels que le *Jardin D'ébène* au Cap, ayant été découvert par ses propriétaires actuelles lors d'un voyage et reflétant leur passion pour ce projet dans le moindre détail, ou le *Chelsea* à Cologne, dans lequel se trouvent partout des œuvres originales d'artistes contemporains que le propriétaire connaît personnellement. Il s'agit également de plus en plus de groupes d'hôtels spécialisés dans la branche des « hôtels économiques », correspondant aux nouvelles attentes de leur clientèle : le souhait de l'originalité et d'un certain facteur de bien-être, loin du design froid et de l'anonymat des chaînes d'hôtels bon marché au charme inexistant.

L'appartenance des différentes maisons de ces nouveaux groupes d'hôtels, telles que l'hôtel *ACE de Palm Springs* ou l'hôtel *Oscar* du groupe espagnol *Room Mate*, ne se voit qu'à moindre mesure, car elles sont conçues tout à fait individuellement et dans le respect de leurs alentours. Aucune chambre d'un même hôtel n'est arrangée de la même façon. Les concepts de base de ces hôtels varient énormément. Ils ont toutefois quelque chose en commun : un caractère particulier. Alex Calderwood, l'un des fondateurs et créateurs du groupe d'hôtels ACE basé à Seattle, établit sa stratégie sur une devise très facile : « simple, basique, confortable ». Cette déclaration reste toutefois en deçà de la réalité, lorsque l'on considère les prestations proposée. C'est une erreur de n'attendre qu'un service correspondant au faible prix. En effet, le wifi gratuit, le service de chambre, les petits restaurants et bars à la mode ne sont pas quelque chose de rare dans ces hôtels.

« Toute vie est résolution de problèmes », comme le déclare la philosophie. Et chaque solution promet une amélioration.

Il semble que nous devons reconnaître une amélioration marquante dans l'hôtellerie. Si vous voulez que votre séjour à l'hôtel se rapproche d'une expérience inoubliable, sans payer une fortune pour cela, vous avez aujourd'hui toutes les chances de votre côté.

Patricia Massó

Introducción

Hay muchos hoteles pagables. Pero quien espera más que sólo una posibilidad de pernoctar entre dos reuniones y que cuando viaja siempre busca algo especial, no sienta su criterio solamente respecto al precio.

Por suerte los hay – hoteles pagables donde al momento de llegar ya se ingresa a un ambiente muy especial e inmediatamente se familiariza con su residencia temporal. A menudo son los hoteles pequeños con administración privada, cuyos propietarios han marcado personalmente el estilo de la casa, tales como el *Jardin D'ébène* en Ciudad del Cabo que fue descubierto por sus actuales propietarios durante un viaje de vacaciones y donde se refleja la pasión por este proyecto con todos su detalles, o el *Chelsea* en Colonia, donde en todas partes están colgadas obras originales de artistas contemporáneos con los cuales el propietario tiene un contacto personal. Sin embargo, los grupos de hoteles también se han especializado cada vez más en el segmento hotelero "a precios cómodos" y se han unido a los mismos para satisfacer las nuevas exigencias de su clientela: el deseo de originalidad y de un cierto factor de bienestar, escapar del diseño demasiado frío y del anonimato de hoteles de cadena baratos sin ningún encanto. En cada uno de los edificios de estos grupos de hoteles nuevos, tales como el *ACE Hotel Palm Springs* o el hotel Oscar del grupo de hoteles *Room Mate* solamente se nota su afinidad de manera limitada, porque fueron concebidos de manera muy individual y prestando atención al vínculo con su entorno correspondiente. Ni siquiera las habitaciones de un solo hotel tienen el mismo equipamiento. Los conceptos que sirven de base para estos hoteles son muy diferentes. Pero tienen algo en común – el carácter muy particular de cada uno. Alex Calderwood, uno de los fundadores y creativos del grupo hotelero ACE, encuentra un denominador común más sencillo para su estrategia: "Simple, básico, cómodo". No obstante, en vista de los servicios ofrecidos, esta afirmación parece subestimada. Quien tema que deba esperar solamente un servicio magro por tal precio, se equivoca. WIFI gratuito, servicio en la habitación (room service), restaurantes pequeños y bares de moda no son raros en estos hoteles.

"Vivir es resolver problemas" – esta es una antigua cognición filosófica. Y cada solución promete un mejoramiento.

Eso parece, también en la hotelería hemos notado un mejoramiento notable. Quien quiera combinar su estadía en el hotel también con una experiencia inolvidable, sin tener que pagar para ello una pequeña fortuna, tiene hoy en día las mejores oportunidades.

Patricia Massó

Introduzione

Di hotel a prezzi accessibili ce ne sono molti. Ma chi si aspetta di più che una semplice possibilità di pernottamento fra un appuntamento e l'altro, ed anche quando viaggia cerca sempre qualche cosa di particolare, non pone soltanto il prezzo come criterio.

Per fortuna esistono – hotel a prezzi accessibili, nei quali già al momento dell'entrata ci si immerge subito in un'atmosfera tutta particolare e si fa amicizia al primo colpo con la propria temporanea dimora. Si tratta spesso degli hotel più piccoli, a gestione privata, dove i proprietari hanno creato personalmente lo stile della casa, come il *Jardin D'ébène* a Città del Capo, che è stato scoperto dalle attuali proprietarie durante una vacanza e nel quale in tutti i suoi dettagli si rispecchia la passione per questo progetto, o il *Chelsea* a Colonia, nel quale sono appese ovunque opere originali di artisti contemporanei con cui il proprietario è in contatto personalmente. Tuttavia, moltissimi sono anche i gruppi di hotel che si sono specializzati sempre più nella fascia "di prezzo accessibile" e che hanno iniziato ad andare incontro alle nuove esigenze della loro clientela: il desiderio di originalità e di un certo fattore benessere, lontano dal design troppo freddo e dall'anonimato di economiche catene di hotel privi di fascino proprio. Per quanto riguarda i singoli hotel di questi nuovi gruppi, come ad esempio l'*ACE Hotel Palm Springs* o l'*Hotel Oscar* del gruppo spagnolo *Room Mate*, la loro affinità si nota solo parzialmente, poiché sono stati concepiti in modo fortemente individuale e tenendo in considerazione il loro rapporto con i rispettivi ambienti. Neanche le stanze di un singolo hotel presentano lo stesso arredamento. I concetti posti alla base di questi hotel sono molto differenziati. Ma hanno una cosa in comune: il carattere di volta in volta assolutamente individuale. Alex Calderwood, uno dei fondatori e dei creativi del gruppo di hotel ACE di Seattle, porta la sua strategia ad un denominatore ancora più semplice: "Semplice, basico, confortevole". Tuttavia la sua affermazione sembra riduttiva, se si tiene conto delle prestazioni offerte. Chi teme di doversi aspettare, visto il prezzo ridotto, un servizio anch'esso di basso livello, sbaglia. Non è un caso raro trovare in questi hotel WIFI gratuito, servizio in camera, piccoli ristoranti e bar.

"Tutta la vita è risolvere problemi", è un'antica nozione filosofica. Ed ogni soluzione annuncia un miglioramento.

Sembra che anche nel settore alberghiero si abbia registrato un notevole miglioramento. Chi ha piacere di far coincidere la propria permanenza in hotel con un'esperienza indimenticabile, senza spendere per questo un piccolo patrimonio, ha oggigiorno le migliori possibilità.

Patricia Massó

ACE Hotel Seattle

2423 First Avenue
Seattle, WA 98121
USA
Phone: +1 / 206 / 4 48 47 21
Fax: +1 / 206 / 3 74 07 45
www.acehotel.com/seattle

Price category: $$
Rooms: 28 rooms
Facilities: Restaurant, café, bar
Services: Free WiFi, pet-friendly
Located: Near downtown, within walking distance of many popular destinations like the Space Needle, Pike Place Market, and the Seattle Waterfront
Public transportation: 1st and Wall
Map: No. 1
Style: Bohemian, organic and hip design
What's special: Hip eco-friendly boutique hotel located near downtown within walking distance of many popular destinations like the Seattle Waterfront and Space Needle. Cyclops Café and the Panther Room bar downstairs serve food and drinks until late at night.

Good Hotel

112 7th Street
San Francisco, CA 94103
USA
Phone: +1 / 415 / 6 21 70 01
Fax: +1 / 415 / 6 21 40 69
www.jdvhotels.com

Price category: $
Rooms: 117 rooms
Facilities: Pizza restaurant serving artisan-style pizzas using only fresh and local ingredients
Services: Parking available, business stations in the lobby, high-speed internet access, pet friendly, outdoor heated pool, bicycles available (for free)
Located: South of Market Street, in the SOMA district
Public transportation: Market St & 7th St
Map: No. 2
Style: Modern, hip design
What's special: Hip hotel located in the SOMA district—one of San Francisco's youngest and most stylish areas. Featuring an eco-friendly décor and practicing: a philanthropic and positive approach "that is designed to inspire the good in us all."

Mosaic

125 Spalding Drive
Beverly Hills, CA 90212
USA
Phone: +1 / 310 / 2 78 03 03
Fax: +1 / 310 / 2 78 17 28
www.mosaichotel.com

Price category: $$
Rooms: 49 rooms
Facilities: Restaurant, heated pool, sports activity center
Services: Internet access, Bose stereo systems with iPod connections
Located: At the heart of Beverly Hills, the Pacific Ocean is only 15 min away at Santa Monica Beach
Map: No. 3
Style: Art Deco and modern classic
Special features: An intimate atmosphere awaits its guests at the Mosaic Hotel—only a short walk away from world-class restaurants, museums, nightclubs and Rodeo Drive. The restaurant and a tropic garden with heated pool offer the perfect relaxation amongst the surrounding attractions.

The Standard Downtown LA

550 South Flower at Sixth Street
Los Angeles, CA 90071
USA
Phone: +1 / 213 / 8 92 80 80
Fax: +1 / 213 / 8 92 86 86
www.standardhotels.com/los-angeles/

Price category: $$
Rooms: 207 rooms
Facilities: 24 h restaurant with outdoor patio, red astro-turf sundeck with waterbed cabanas, indoor lobby lounge with billiards, heated rooftop pool and poolbar
Services: Free WiFi, video games, DVD player, 24 h room service, photo booth, valet parking
Located: In downtown Los Angeles
Public transportation: 7th Street / Metro Center Station
Map: No. 4
Style: Contemporary design
What's special: Extravagant 207 room hotel decorated with a unique mix of modern and retro elements located in the business district downtown LA. The rooftop pool and bar situated amidst the tops of the skyscrapers is an attractive meeting point for a drink.

CITY NATIONAL BANK

ACE Hotel Palm Springs

701 E. Palm Canyon Dr
Palm Springs, CA 92264
USA
Phone: +1 / 760 / 3 25 99 00
Fax: +1 / 760 / 3 25 78 78
www.acehotel.com/palmsprings

Price category: $$
Rooms: 180 rooms
Facilities: Bar, restaurant, swim club (including a pool, hot tub, spa, gym, massage yurts, hammocks, and a stargazing deck)
Services: Free WiFi, gym, room service, dog-friendly, free bikes, scooter rentals
Located: Walking distance to downtown Palm Springs
Public transportation: East Palm Canyon
Map: No. 5
Style: Bohemian, organic and hip design
What's special: Bohemian-style hotel built on the grounds of a renovated mid-century modern motel. The eco-friendly hotel features rooms with a garden patio or fireplace and communal fireplaces throughout the hotel. The perfect place to stay for a desert holiday.

Hotel St. Francis

210 Don Gaspar Avenue
Santa Fe, NM 87501
USA
Phone: +1 / 505 / 9 83 57 00
Fax: +1 / 505 / 9 89 76 90
www.hotelstfrancis.com

Price category: $$
Rooms: 81 rooms
Facilities: Bar, restaurant, spa, conference and wedding facilities, fitness room
Services: Weddings and business service, WiFi
Located: One block southwest of the historic Plaza and within walking distance of museums, shops, and galleries
Public transportation: At the historic Plaza: Rail Runner train and city
Map: No. 6
Style: Victorian style, rustic luxury
What's special: Tranquil and peaceful hotel providing moments for reflection and contemplation located one block from the historic Santa Fe Plaza and in walking distance to other local attractions. The design is inspired by the early presence of the Franciscan missionaries in New Mexico.

Catalina Hotel & Beach Club

1720 - 1756 Collins Avenue
Miami Beach, FL 33139
USA
Phone: +1 / 305 / 6 74 11 60
Fax: +1 / 305 / 6 72 82 16
www.catalinasouthbeach.com

Price category: $
Rooms: 192 rooms
Facilities: Bistro, bar, restaurant, bamboo pool, rooftop pool, beach club, gym
Services: Free WiFi, iPod docking station, airport shuttle, free bikes and beach chairs, free Happy Hour cocktails
Located: In the heart of South Beach
Public transportation: Collins Av/18 St
Map: No. 7
Style: Eclectic style
What's special: This true historic South Beach non-smoking hotel with its own nightclub offers affordable luxury in a stylish and sophisticated environment.
Two rooftop pools, three bars and lounges and two restaurants guarantee a dazzling time for all guests who stay in the hotel.

USA
Phone: +1 / 561 / 8 32 00 94
Fax: +1 / 561 / 8 33 78 48
www.hotelbiba.com

Facilities: Wine bar, garden
Services: WiFi, champagner and house parties, jazz nights
Located: At the heart of the historic district in West Palm Beach
Public transportation: Palm Tran bus station
Map: No. 8
Style: Modern and historic, funky
What's special: Once among the first motor lodges in the United State the Biba was later redesigned by Barbara Hulanicki, the famous fashion designer of the Sixties in London. The mix of historic architecture and playful modern interior design and the serene garden with pool make it a real retreat at the heart of West Palm Beach.

The Standard New York

848 Washington Street
New York, NY 10014
USA
Phone: +1 / 212 / 6 45 46 46
Fax: +1 / 212 / 6 45 56 56
www.standardhotels.com/new-york-city

Price category: $$
Rooms: 337 rooms and suites
Facilities: Restaurants "The Standard Grill", "The Living-room", and Biergarten Bar
Services: Free WiFi, fully-equipped venues for private events, iPod ready sound system, 24 h room service
Located: Between Meatpacking district and West Village
Public transportation: 8th Ave-14th
Map: No. 9
Style: Eclectic mix with elements from the '50s to the '70s on different floors
What's special: Ultrachic hotel standing on the historical High Line in the Meatpacking District in Lower Manhattan next to the Hudson river and in walking distance to shopping and cultural sites. All rooms have ground to ceiling windows with spectacular views.

Habita Monterrey

Vasconcelos No. 150 OTE
San Pedro, Garza Garcia
Nuevo Leon
Mexico, CP 66220
Phone: +52 / 81 / 83 35 59 00
Fax: +52 / 81 / 83 35 09 99
www.hotelhabitamty.com

Price category: $$
Rooms: 39 rooms
Facilities: Rooftop terrace pool and bar, restaurant, bar, business center, gym, spa, shops, complimentary AUDI service upon request
Services: WiFi, X-box, 24 h room service, valet parking, airport shuttle service
Located: In the business center of Monterrey
Map: No. 10
Style: Contemporary design
What's special: Minimalistic chic boutique hotel with 39 luxury rooms and notable rooftop terrace with fantastic views of the Monterrey cityscape and the mountains. The hotel features stunning public spaces and is placed in the most exclusive area of Monterrey, surrounded by high end shopping boutiques and restaurants.

CONDESA*df*

Avenida Veracruz N.102
Colonia Condesa
Mexico, DF 06700
Phone: +52 / 55 / 52 41 26 00
Fax: +52 / 55 / 52 41 26 40
www.condesadf.com

Price category: $$
Rooms: 40 rooms and suites
Facilities: Congress and meeting rooms, terrace, patio, bar, restaurant, cinema, dancefloor
Services: 24 h room service, DVD player, iPod, high speed internet, airport shuttle service
Located: In a safe, central residential area of Mexico City, 5–10 min walking distance to bars, restaurants, museums and boutiques around
Map: No. 11
Style: Sophisticated, contemporary
What's special: Stylish and fun chic in a remodeled mansion reflecting its neighbourhood perfectly—fashionable and trendy, yet respectful and traditional. The rooftop terrace, the Turkish steam room, and a thermal bath are an invitation for ultimate relaxation.

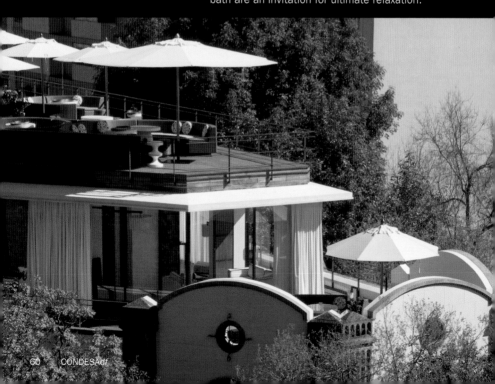

Pousada Picinguaba

Vila Picinguaba, Rua G, 130
11680-000 Ubatuba-SP
State of São Paulo
Brazil
Phone: +55 / 12 / 38 36 91 05
Fax: +55 / 12 / 38 36 91 03
www.picinguaba.com

Price category: $$
Rooms: 9 double rooms and 1 honeymoon suite
Facilities: Restaurant, private schooner, pool, home theater, sauna, private villas, tropical garden
Services: Transportation and guide services, massages
Located: Half-way between Rio and São Paulo, in a peaceful bay at the heart of a Natural Park
Public transportation: Bus: Rio de Janeiro, Novo Rio to Paraty or São Paulo, Rodoviaria Tietê, to Ubatuba
Map: No. 12
Style: Rustic and charming
What's special: Exceptional hideaway comprising 10 rooms on a 3 km-long protected beach a 3 ½ hour scenic drive away from both Rio de Janeiro and São Paulo. Relaxed and open-minded atmosphere in the heart of the Mata Atlantica rainforest—a unique eco-system.

Bo Bo

Guatemala 4882
Palermo Soho C1425BUP
Buenos Aires
Argentina
Phone: +54 / 11 / 47 74 05 05
Fax: +54 / 11 / 47 74 96 00
www.bobohotel.com

Price category: $$
Rooms: 15 rooms
Facilities: Restaurant, bar, spa services
Services: Room service, internet
Located: In the heart of the Palermo district, close to trendy bars and restaurants
Public transportation: Plaza Italia
Map: No. 13
Style: Individually decorated rooms, from classic Argentinean to minimalist desgin
What's special: Set in a renovated old colonial style house in Palermo Viejo—a high-end shopping district with many restaurants about 20 minutes from the dazzling city center—the Bo Bo has 15 individually decorated rooms, some with terrace or patio. The restaurant and bar offer a good selection of wines.

Rex Hotel

Luntmakargatan 73
SE-111 51 Stockholm
Sweden
Phone: +46 / 8 / 16 00 40
Fax: +46 / 8 / 6 61 86 01
www.rexhotel.se

Price category: $$
Rooms: 56 rooms
Facilities: Conference rooms
Services: Free broadband access
Located: In the center of Stockholm
Public transportation: Rådmansgatan
Map: No. 14
Style: Refurbished town house from 1866 with pure design and distinct colors
What's special: Homely-feeling hotel in a refurbished town house from 1866 right in the city center. The design of the hotel and the permanent photo exhibition reflect the owner's artistic and international background. Their philosophy is to provide the traveller with outstanding individual service upon demand.

The Square

Rådhuspladsen 14
1550 Copenhagen V
Denmark
Phone: +45 / 33 / 38 12 00
Fax: +45 / 33 / 38 12 01
www.thesquarecopenhagen.com

Price category: $
Rooms: 267 rooms and suites
Facilities: 2 conference rooms
Services: WiFi in the conference rooms and in the lobby, 24 h reception, room service for breakfast, car rental, high speed internet access
Located: At City Hall Square in the city center
Public transportation: Central Station
Map: No. 15
Style: Fashionable minimalist design
What's special: The elegant minimalist design of the 267 rooms and a warm welcoming atmosphere make The Square an ideal choice for both business and pleasure. The hotel is located in the pulsating center of town; nearly all sights and attractions are close at hand, including the elegant pedestrian shopping street Strøget.

Warwick Barsey Hotel

Avenue Louise 381–383
1050 Brussels
Belgium
Phone: +32 / 2 / 6 49 98 00
Fax: +32 / 2 / 6 40 17 64
www.warwickbarsey.com

Price category: $$
Rooms: 99 rooms
Facilities: Bar, restaurant, 5 meeting rooms
Services: Meeting rooms have ADSL, free in-room LAN internet, concierge, 24 h room service
Located: On prestigious Avenue Louise, in Brussels' fashionable shopping area, and in close proximity to the Bois de la Cambre and the Place du Châtelain
Public transportation: Abbaye
Map: No. 16
Style: A blend of neoclassical and Napoleon III styles
What's special: The elegant and cosy property comprising 99 rooms has been decorated by the famous French designer Jacques García and is situated in Brussels' fashionable shopping area. Every weekend lounge music with live DJ is featured in the restaurant's bar.

Hotel misc

Kloveniersburgwal 20
1012 CV Amsterdam
The Netherlands
Phone: +31 / 20 / 3 30 62 41
Fax: +31 / 20 / 3 30 62 42
www.misceatdrinksleep.com

Price category: $
Rooms: 6 rooms
Facilities: Bar, discount for the botanical garden
Services: Massage, free non-alcoholic drink & snack bar, free WiFi connection, arrangement of walking tours
Located: Close to Nieuwmarkt square, in the center of Amsterdam
Public transportation: Nieuwmarkt
Map: No. 17
Style: Themed rooms with individual style (Design, Wonders, Rembrandt, Retro Africa, Baroque)
What's special: Lovely little hotel located in the heart of the historic city center of Amsterdam. The modernized 17th-century canal house features six personally decorated rooms in a unique mix of style. A perfect place for discovering restaurants, cafés, museums, and shops.

Knightsbridge Hotel

10 Beaufort Gardens
London SW3 1PT
United Kingdom
Phone: +44 / 20 / 75 84 63 00
Fax: +44 / 20 / 75 84 63 55
www.firmdale.com

Price category: $$
Rooms: 44 rooms and suites
Facilities: Each guest area has a working fireplace, drawing room, library (also DVDs)
Services: Concierge, 24 h room service, WiFi access
Located: In the heart of Knightsbridge, the area is filled with some of London's most interesting bars, cafés and restaurants
Public transportation: Knightsbridge
Map: No. 18
Style: Contemporary English
What's special: Located on a quiet, tree-lined street, only a short walk away from Harrods, this English modern-styled boutique hotel is not only a perfect place for shopping and sightseeing but also for enjoying the traditional afternoon tea by the hotel's fireplaces.

Main House

6 Colville Road
London W11 2BP
United Kingdom
Phone: +44 / 20 / 72 21 96 91
Fax: +44 / 20 / 72 21 96 91
www.themainhouse.co.uk

Price category: $
Rooms: 4 rooms and 3 suites
Facilities: Special day rate for Main House guests at Lambton Place for gym, swimming and treatments
Services: Cell phone with answer service and wireless internet connection, transport service, bicycle hire
Located: In Notting Hill, surrounded by famous parks, the Albert Hall, and museums within walking distance
Public transportation: Notting Hill Gate
Map: No. 19
Style: Victorian house, stylishly furnished with antiques
What's special: The smart property is located a step away from the famous Portobello Road with its antique markets, designer shops, and art galleries. Guests of the hotel can have organic breakfast on the balcony.

Hotel Amano

Auguststrasse 43
10119 Berlin
Germany
Phone: +49 / 30 / 8 09 41 50
Fax: +49 / 30 / 80 94 15 22 00
www.hotel-amano.com

Price category: $
Rooms: 163, including 47 apartments
Facilities: Large roof terrace with view over Berlin, bar, boules court in the garden, conference room
Services: Bicycle rental, stereo systems and iPod, personal trainer lessons on request, free W-LAN
Located: In the Mitte district near Hackesche Höfe
Public transportation: Rosenthaler Platz
Map: No. 20
Style: Modern, contemporary
What's special: Pure urban located in a favourable location in Berlin Mitte only some steps from the House of Representatives, Museum island, Alexanderplatz Square and the vibrant Hackescher Markt with shops and restaurants. The hotel's highlight is a large roof terrace with a fantastic view over Berlin.

Hotel La Maison

Occamstrasse 24
80802 Munich
Germany
Phone: +49 / 89 / 33 03 55 50
Fax: +49 / 89 / 3 30 35 55 55
www.hotel-la-maison.com

Price category: $
Rooms: 31 rooms
Facilities: Bar "Blue Hour" and restaurant "Kokoro by Ollysan"
Services: Babysitting, leave and go service for regular customers
Located: In the center of Schwabing, close to the English Garden
Public transportation: Münchner Freiheit
Map: No. 21
Style: Contemporary design
What's special: Small elegant hotel located in the Schwabing district of Munich, next to the English Garden, with a homy feeling. The combined lounge-bar-restaurant area is the place to be for Munich's trendy scene and visitors alike.

Hotel Chelsea

Jülicher Strasse 1
50674 Cologne
Germany
Phone: +49 / 221 / 20 71 50
Fax: +49 / 221 / 23 91 37
www.hotel-chelsea.de

Price category: $
Rooms: 35 rooms, 3 suites, 26 luxury apartments
Facilities: "Café Central", restaurant "o.T.", conference room
Services: Free WiFi, printer free of charge, parking and garage space available on request
Located: In the city center of Cologne
Public transportation: Rudolfplatz
Map: No. 22
Style: Contemporary design
What's special: Privately owned and managed hotel filled with international contemporary art created by artists like Martin Kippenberger and Günther Förg. The oblique construction creates unusual and exciting spaces. Some of the rooms have their own rooftop terrace.

Goldman 25Hours

Hanauer Landstrasse 127
60314 Frankfurt
Germany
Phone: +49 / 69 / 40 58 68 90
Fax: +49 / 69 / 40 58 68 98 90
www.25hours-hotels.com/frankfurt

Price category: $
Rooms: 49 individually decorated guest rooms
Facilities: "Goldman Restaurant", bar, lounge
Services: Free WiFi, jogging corner, iPod sound system
Located: Frankfurt East End, situated among design and furniture stores, creative agencies and insider clubs
Public transportation: Osthafenplatz
Map: No. 23
Style: Eclectic design, vintage aesthetic with fancy details
What's special: Located in Frankfurt's bustling East End district, the funky Goldman 25hours is both a hideaway and a local hot spot featuring a variety of vintage eclecticism and themed rooms. An outdoor terrace offers a South Seas feel on summer nights.

Blaue Gans

Getreidegasse 41–43
5020 Salzburg
Austria
Phone: +43 / 662 / 8 42 49 10
Fax: +43 / 662 / 8 42 49 10
www.blauegans.at

Price category: $$
Rooms: 37 rooms
Facilities: "Restaurant Salzburg", bar, cavern, meeting rooms
Services: Room service, WiFi, dog-friendly
Located: In Salzburg's city center, near Mozart's Birthplace and all major sights
Public transportation: Herbert von Karajan Platz
Map: No. 24
Style: Tradition and innovation: contemporary art and design in a 650 years old building
What's special: The oldest Inn in town with a 650 year old tradition was carefully reconstructed in 2002. The co-existence of the historic Austrian heritage and innovation makes this art hotel located in the city center of Salzburg a charming home.

La Maison Bordeaux

113, Rue Albert Barraud
33000 Bordeaux
France
Phone: +33 / 5 / 56 44 00 45
Fax: +33 / 5 / 56 44 17 31
www.lamaisonbord-eaux.com

Price category: $
Rooms: All 6 rooms view on the garden
Facilities: Wine bar "Grands Crus", meeting rooms
Services: Breakfast and meals are served in the garden in summer, internet access in the rooms, free tea and coffee
Located: In the very heart of Bordeaux
Public transportation: Martin
Map: No. 25
Style: Comfortable, contemporary
What's special: Contemporary decorated boutique hotel located in the heart of Bordeaux with 6 stylish decorated rooms overlooking the garden. The owners belong to a family of famous winegrowers and offer a large range of wines in the restaurant and the bar.

Bourg Tibourg

19, Rue du Bourg-Tibourg
75004 Paris
France
Phone: +33 / 1 / 42 78 47 39
Fax: +33 / 1 / 40 29 07 00
www.hotelbourgtibourg.com

Price category: $$
Rooms: 30 rooms
Facilities: Bar, garden
Services: Handicapped access, restaurants, shows, WiFi, parking near the hotel, DVD player
Located: In the heart of the Marais district, walking distance to historic cultural Paris
Public transportation: Hôtel de Ville
Map: No. 26
Style: Neogothic with oriental influences
What's special: Cosy intimate rooms and a warm and welcoming atmosphere await guests in this charming townhouse decorated by Jacques García. Located in the heart of the Marais district it is the perfect starting point for discovering historical Paris and the cafés and restaurants of this trendy area.

Casa della Palma

Via dei Sabelli 98
00185 Rome, San Lorenzo
Italy
Phone: +39 / 06 / 4 45 42 64
Fax: +39 / 06 / 2 33 24 55 62
www.casadellapalma.it

Price category: $
Rooms: 8 rooms and one loft for 5 people
Facilities: Rooftop terrace, green inner courtyard
Services: Free city bikes, internet access in all rooms
Located: In the trendy San Lorenzo district
Public transportation: Reti
Map: No. 27
Style: Romantic-industrial
What's special: A quiet retreat with a relaxing green courtyard located in the bustling area of San Lorenzo on the east side of the ancient walls surrounded by many restaurants and bars. Individually decorated rooms and a personal service make this townhouse-style hotel feel like a comfortable private Italian home.

Townhouse 12

Piazza Gerusalemme 12
20154 Milan,
Zona Corso Sempione
Italy
Phone: +39 / 02 / 89 07 85 11
Fax: +39 / 02 / 89 07 85 17
www.townhouse.it

Price category: $$
Rooms: 18 rooms
Facilities: Terrace bar and lobby bar
Services: Meeting room
Located: Close to the trade fair
Public transportation: Procaccini Lomazzo
Map: No. 28
Style: Minimalistic
What's special: Chic hotel with relaxing atmosphere located in central Milan near Corso Sempione and the Fieramilano City exposition centre comprising 15 tastefully furnished bedrooms, some of them with private balcony or terrace.

Room Mate Oscar

Plaza Vázquez de Mella 12
28004 Madrid
Spain
Phone: +34 / 917 / 01 11 73
Fax: +34 / 915 / 21 62 96
www.room-matehotels.com

Price category: $
Rooms: 75 rooms
Facilities: Restaurant "Gift"
Services: Free WiFi, personal service, meeting rooms, babysitting service and medical attention upon request
Located: Next to Gran Vía, in one of the most luminous plazas of Madrid's downtown
Public transportation: Gran Vía
Map: No. 29
Style: Avant-garde
What's special: Thanks to its proximity to the city's most important museums like the Prado and the Thyssen Bornemisza as well as to the historic centre's restaurants, Madrid's top theatres and cinemas and to the shopping district, the cosmopolitan Oscar is the ideal place to be in Madrid.

ÓSCAR
Iloveroommate™
Ilovenewyorkmiamibuenosairesbarcelonamexicocityparismadridrioamsterdam
Room Mate

Hotel Soho Barcelona

Gran Vía, 543–545
08011 Barcelona, Eixample
Spain
Phone: +34 / 935 / 52 96 10
Fax: +34 / 935 / 52 96 11
www.hotelsohobarcelona.com

Price category: $
Rooms: 51 rooms
Facilities: Lounge, terrace, outdoor pool
Services: Conference room for up to 20 people
Located: In the Eixample district
Public transportation: Urgell
Map: No. 30
Style: Contemporary design
What's special: As one of the most sophisticated hotels in all of Barcelona, Hotel Soho is a bit of downtown New York on the fabulous Gran Vía Avenue. Designed by Alfredo Arribas, this 51 room luxury boutique hotel is perfect for business and pleasure travelers alike. The rooftop terrace and pool is a great place to spend a sunny afternoon.

Solar do Castelo

Rua das Cozinhas, 2 (ao Castelo)
1100-181 Lisbon
Portugal
Phone: +351 / 218 / 80 60 50
Fax: +351 / 218 / 87 09 07
www.heritage.pt

Price category: $
Rooms: 14 rooms
Facilities: Medieval remains and a small garden
Services: Free high speed WiFi, 24 h room service, DVD library, concierge, turndown service
Located: Within the walls of the São Jorge Castle, in the heart of Lisbon historic center
Public transportation: Castelo
Map: No. 31
Style: Medieval contemporary
What's special: Originally built in the XVIIIth century this former mansion is hosting a charming and calm boutique hotel in the historic center of Lisbon. The elements of medieval times featured everywhere in the hotel decorated in a mix of medieval and contemporary style pay tribute to the rich past of this small palace.

Ajia Hotel

Ahmet Rasim Paca Yalisi,
Cubuklu Cad. No. 27
Kanlica Istanbul
Turkey
Phone: +90 / 216 / 4 13 93 00
Fax: +90 / 216 / 4 13 93 55
www.ajiahotel.com

Price category: $$
Rooms: 15 rooms and suites
Facilities: Restaurant, meeting room, 5 rooms with private balcony, suites with jakuzzi
Services: Outdoor banquet organizations, boat shuttle, private dining and weddings organizations, private airport transfer, massage
Located: On the shores of Bosphorus in Kanlıca, on the Asian part of Istanbul
Public transportation: Çubuklu
Map: No. 32
Style: Contemporary
What's special: Individually minimalistic decorated rooms feature a warm and calm atmosphere and reflect the mix of tradition and modernity.

Riad 72

72 Arset Awsel
Bab Doukkala Marrakech
Morocco
Phone: +212 / 24 / 38 76 29
Fax: +212 / 24 / 38 47 18
www.riad72.com

Price category: $$
Rooms: 4 rooms
Facilities: Restaurant, bookshop featuring arts and handicrafts
Services: The whole riad can be rented on an exclusive basis for groups of 8 to 12 persons, yoga, massage, private event organizations
Located: In the Old City of Marrakech, in a pedestrian street in the famous Dar El Bacha antiquities district
Map: No. 33
Style: Traditional hospitality boutique
What's special: Intimate 4-bedroom riad furnished in a mix of contemporary and traditional style. The patio with banana trees and a panoramic roof terrace with views over the city invite to have a glass of mint tea.

Grand Daddy

38 Long Street
Cape Town, 8001
South Africa
Phone: +27 / 21 / 4 24 72 47
Fax: +27 / 21 / 4 24 72 48
www.granddaddy.co.za

Price category: $$
Rooms: 26 rooms and 7 rooms in the trailers
Facilities: Airstream Penthouse Trailer Park, restaurant, bar, cinema, meeting rooms
Services: Room service, fully serviced
Located: In the Cape Town city center, located between sea and Table Mountain
Public transportation: Cape Town Railway Station
Map: No. 34
Style: Modern, contemporary
What's special: A place with a creative ambiance in the middle of Cape Town. A surprise is awaiting the guests on the rooftop of the hotel: A collection of seven vintage Airstream caravans nestled beneath the backdrop of Table Mountain, conceptualized and designed by local artists—an accommodation like no other.

Jardin D'ébène

21 Warren Street, Tamboerskloof
Cape Town, 8001
South Africa
Phone: +27 / 21 / 4 26 10 11
Fax: +27 / 21 / 4 22 24 23
www.jardindebene.co.za

Price category: $$
Rooms: 4 rooms
Facilities: Plunge pool, sundeck
Services: Free WiFi
Located: In the heart of the City Bowl, right below Table Mountain, 5 min. walking distance from trendy Kloof Street
Map: No. 35
Style: Contemporary African style
What's special: Elegant South African townhouse with plungepool and sundeck decorated in a contemporary African style. The tranquil property comprises five elegant bedrooms situated around a lounge and is located right below the Table Mountain in the heart of Cape Town's City Bowl.

Media One Hotel Dubai

Dubai Media City, Plot no. 1
Behind American University
Dubai
United Arab Emirates
Phone: +971 / 4 / 4 27 10 00
Fax: +971 / 4 / 4 27 10 01
www.mediaonehotel.com

Price category: $$
Rooms: 260 rooms including 10 suites
Facilities: Fully equipped gym, steam and sauna rooms, pool and sundeck, 2 bars and 3 restaurants, outside "Chill-Out" lounge, grill and bar
Services: High-speed WiFi, iPod docking station
Located: In the center of the Media City district
Public transportation: Dubai Media City
Map: No. 36
Style: Trendy and contemporary
What's special: Stylish urban property occupying the first 23 floors of a 43 story building in the Media City district in Dubai designed with the savvy business traveller in mind. The restaurant, chillout café and bar are also a favourite option for professionals based in and around Media City.

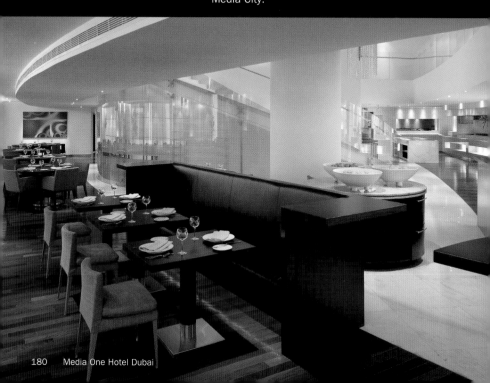

JIA Hong Kong

1–5 Irving Street, Causeway Bay
Hong Kong
Phone: +852 / 3196 / 90 00
Fax: +852 / 3196 / 90 01
www.jiahongkong.com

Price category: $$
Rooms: 54 rooms
Facilities: Italian restaurant & bar, Tapas Bar, high-tech conference rooms, open air podium
Services: Complimentary broadband/WiFi, DVD/VCD player
Located: In the Causeway Bay area, nearby shopping areas with restaurants
Public transportation: Causeway Bay
Map: No. 37
Style: The hippest hotel in Hong Kong, stylish and urban, designed by Philippe Starck
What's special: The first boutique hotel in Asia is located in the buzzing shopping and entertainment district on Hong Kong Island. All rooms are designed as a residence and come with a kitchen. The Open-air podium and sundeck features facilities for entertaining and barbeque.

JIA Shanghai

931 West Nanjing Road
(Entrance on Taixing Road)
Shanghai 200041
China
Phone: +86 / 21 / 62 17 90 00
Fax: +86 / 21 / 62 87 90 01
www.jiashanghai.com

Price category: $$
Rooms: 55 studio rooms and suites, including a rock-star Penthouse suite
Facilities: Techno gym, Italian restaurant & bar
Services: Complimentary broadband/wifi, suites with personal bartender
Located: In the heart of Shanghai, surrounded by shopping and entertainment delights
Public transportation: Nanjing Xi Lu
Map: No. 38
Style: Playful, cool, hip, intimate and high privacy
What's special: Residential-style designer boutique hotel set in a 1920's building in the heart of Shanghai. The concept is striking a perfect balance between a home and a hotel and all rooms are fitted with fully equipped kitchens and the latest communication technology.

Shanghai Mansion

479–481 Yaowaraj Road
Samphantawong
Bangkok 10100
Thailand
Phone: + 66 / 22 21 / 21 21
Fax: + 66 / 22 21 / 21 24
www.shanghaimansion.com

Price category: $$
Rooms: 60 superior and deluxe rooms and 16 suites
Facilities: Cotton Jazz Bar, spa, library, internet corner
Services: Room service, free WiFi, shuttle Tuk Tuk to major attractions, airport transfer, baby cot upon request
Located: In Bangkok's historic Chinatown district
Public transportation: Hua Lamphong
Map: No. 39
Style: Intimate, oriental glamour, hip design hotel
What's special: Seductive Chinese-style rooms revoking an elegant mansion in 1930's glamorous Shanghai. The building was one of the first nine-story buildings in the early Chinatown community, today known as Bangkok's historic Chinatown district and was originally owned by one of the country's most prominent old Thai-Chinese families and was once a Chinese opera house.

dusitD2 chiang mai

100 Chang Klan Road,
Tambol Chang Klan
Amphur Muang, Chiang Mai, 50100
Thailand
Phone: +66 / 53 99 / 99 99
Fax: +66 / 53 99 / 99 00
www.dusit.com/d2cm

Price category: $$
Rooms: 131 rooms
Facilities: Restaurant, bar, health club, spa, outdoor pool
Services: High-speed internet access, concierge, baby-sitting, express laundry, transport by D2 van and private limousine
Located: In the heart of downtown Chiang Mai
Public transportation: Tuk Tuk and Song Taew
Map: No. 40
Style: Warm chic interior, contemporary urban Thai design
What's special: Chic and well equipped hotel in a contemporary Thai design located in the heart of downtown Chiang Mai. Several business facilities such as the outdoor pool and the spa—one of the best-equipped health clubs in Chiang Mai—make the hotel the ideal place for both, business and leisure.

The Hatton

65 Park Street
South Yarra 3141
Melbourne
Australia
Phone: +61 / 3 / 98 68 48 00
Fax: +61 / 3 / 98 68 48 99
www.hatton.com.au

Price category: $$
Rooms: 20 deluxe suites
Facilities: Roof terrace, lounge bar, meeting room
Services: Wi-fi, express laundry facility, massage, meeting rooms
Located: In residential South Yarra, close to the botanic gardens
Public transportation: Toorak Rd/Park St
Map: No. 41
Style: Comfort and functionality with sophisticated contemporary Melbourne style
What's special: Sophisticated boutique hotel rich in Italianate period features decorated in a mix of traditional and contemporary local furniture and decorative artworks reflecting the cross cultural diversity and history of Melbourne.

Vibe Hotel Sydney

111 Goulburn Street,
Sydney, NSW 2000
Australia
Phone: +61 / 2 / 82 72 33 00
Fax: +61 / 2 / 92 11 18 06
www.vibehotels.com.au

Price category: $$
Rooms: 190 guest rooms, including 6 suites
Facilities: Sauna, rooftop heated swimming pool, bar, café, conference venues, restaurant
Services: Foxtel & in-room movies, in-room broadband access (charges apply), business services
Located: In the heart of Sydney
Public transportation: Museum Station
Map: No. 42
Style: Unique style, vibrant atmosphere
What's special: Chic accommodation in the heart of Sydney perfectly positioned only a few minutes away from Sydney's premier tourist destinations like Sydney Centrepoint Tower, Darling Harbour, Hyde Park, The Rocks and Circular Quay—the perfect location for discovering the city.

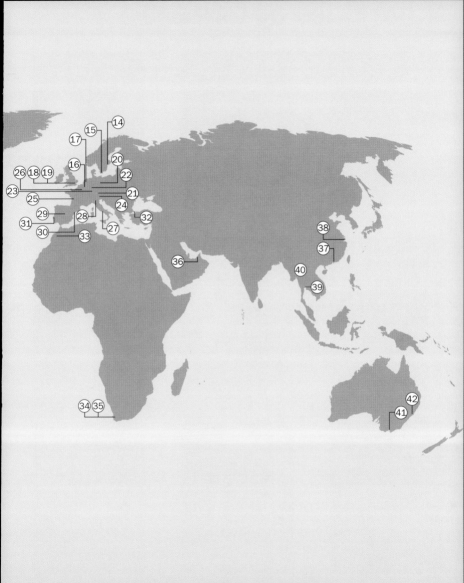

Other titles by teNeues

ISBN 978-3-8327-9309-8

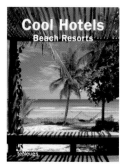

ISBN 978-3-8327-9274-9

ISBN 978-3-8327-9237-4

ISBN 978-3-8327-9247-3

ISBN 978-3-8327-9234-3

ISBN 978-3-8327-9308-1

ISBN 978-3-8327-9243-5

ISBN 978-3-8327-9230-5

ISBN 978-3-8327-9396-8

Size: **15 x 19 cm**, 6 x 7 ½ in., 224 pp., **Flexicover**, c. 200 color photographs,
Text: English / German / French / Spanish / Italian
www.teneues.com

Other titles by teNeues

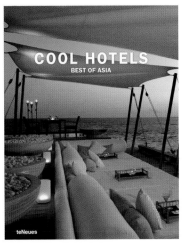

ISBN 978-3-8327-9238-1

ISBN 978-3-8327-9235-0

Size: **25.6 x 32.6 cm**, 10 x 12⅞ in., 396 pp., **Hardcover with jacket**, c. 650 color photographs,
Text: English / German / French / Spanish / Italian
www.teneues.com

teNeues' new Cool Guide series

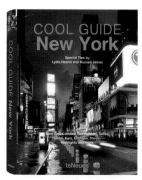

ISBN 978-3-8327-9293-0

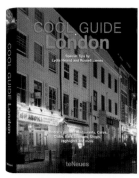

ISBN 978-3-8327-9294-7

ISBN 978-3-8327-9295-4

ISBN 978-3-8327-9296-1

ISBN 978-3-8327-9236-7

ISBN 978-3-8327-9202-2

Size: **15 x 19 cm**, 6 x 7 ½ in., 224 pp., **Flexicover**, c. 250 color photographs,
Text: English / German / French / Spanish

www.teneues.com